Earth
Hannah Brooks-Motl

The Song Cave

The Song Cave
www.the-song-cave.com
© Hannah Brooks-Motl, 2019
Cover image: © Kraus Rinke

Design and layout by Janet Evans-Scanlon

ISBN: 978-0-578-51437-6
Library of Congress Control Number: 2019943429

FIRST EDITION

Then must be realized no harmony but a system of discrepancies beautiful as the rotted peach.

MARGUERITE YOUNG,
Angel in the Forest

Contents

Letter from Wong May   1

Living   5

Idyll   11

Spell   13

Through   15

Mansions   19

Parable   25

Earth   30

Bucolic   31

The Pencil   35

Going   38

Ode   45

Virtue Theory   50

Poetry   88

Capitol   93

Acknowledgments   97

Hannah—

*I was sitting beside you on a muddy riverbank, & woke with the scent of water &
mud, we have been to parties, visited houses etc., there was a horse, there was
fleetingly your brother, the neighbours, you growing up into the woman not killed
by the girl, into a poet, also the pre-natal—"hiding in a rural place & being
born"—I have been climbing the tree of language with you, its many levels, look-
ing up & down, inspecting bird nests, apples, crab apple—yes, all neither here nor
there—the place is not important, nor time being the dream that it was, from
reading you late into the night. But the voice & the other noises, all the going-
ons—go on.*

*What I like is—beside your voice, the other noises one hears off the page, "sure
that the sentence rots when no ones in it."*

*So the peach rotted is rotting & beautiful—full of death but not dead, at least as
seen. I love the physicality, all the particulars that make your generalisations
JUMP & hold true.*

*Didn't Keats say being a poet one lives one's life allegorically. I think it goes with
a way of seeing, what makes a scene alive in a glance (it has to—one is granted
no other moment) is what makes an aphorism. Above all it is TERROR—of
seeing/ or even more heart-stoppingly—being.*

"The teacher & the dune joined at the pencil."

*I can garner many such beyond memorable lines—still neater than an aphorism,
this is an equation. It is edifying/ electrifying, so your poems pulse with delights
& surprises, it is a giddy reading experience. At times giggly. I say edifying as
well, "Nature planted root vegetables, performed life from memory"—*

*There is an intelligence that informs the words, an engagement with language,
always with great tact & suppleness—"to tinker with matter," the heart of the*

matter, which is poetry, though the subject is still the poet's sensibility, & you couldn't be more serious about the subject matter, a poet's primal responsibility is with language. The struggle of "words are difficult to put into the words"—& your vocabulary felicitously matches your attention to the world.

"The mirror is majestic & raw & just like biology"

Now this statement defines—for me, in a frame, the TERROR (of seeing)— e.g. the butchered bodies of Francis Bacon & Chaim Soutine.

& what aplomb!!—

"A person in casual shoes walking to their local meaning"

"A man stood next to his heart"

& the iconic immediacy of

*"A broken orange
settled on the mud"*

& the static/ iconic,

*"Sirens, icons
Bacon, eggs"*

Is poetry the screen before the altar?

—Wong May

Living

Barely lived in the house it was written about, I didn't
have rituals. Couldn't help the past,
its deeper zones and practices. Its elite visions.
And time was a friend, a rival.

People struggled through the ratio—
what do you remember about it?
It was a garland of lilies stitched into fabric.
There was a spirit named Impudence
to fall in love with. There were three potheads
out in the dark; a curtain tacked up as a door.

And within the joy of amateurs.
Is daring healthy, or boredom?
And giving everyone their space as an ideology.
Taking apart the song
for the sadness of pleasure.
That tribute but other debts too.
Taking apart the song.
Being alone with one's bottle.
Was this the whole world poet?

Didn't have the basic information
so I invented myself.
And the real or its insinuation was somewhere
beyond all that. What was it like for you there?

It was sparsely attended. All language
was anonymous; everyone was farmers
or nurses. At night they sat on low futons.
There was a demon called Consequence
the Extinguisher, I remember her golden scarves.

It was strange about the translucence
of individuals, what people said
to one another. Orange plush.

The attic grew colder.

Could you identify the desolation? Pain is not
commensurate but one is bitter
making up the day. Many of us loved
the rural walks and dead historian of science,
everyone filmed the present. Spreading reddish.
Someone brought a gun.

Begging her child to tell a story in the painting
of the painting. What's the fancy term for that?

It was brave to arrive at the inner conclusions,
the hallways smelling of indeterminate spice
when you left me. Where did you go?
On the balcony with a jewel.
In the well-litness of the lonely.

Imagine the highways had been made
of love, all the highways
and intimate townscapes.
Into cranberry color
of car light and dawning.

There were couches out front
—orange plush, then flannel—
that used to be beds.

There was a house of god on the way.
And flowering weeds—orange, orange, and umber.
Kids pulling wagons through dirt. I pressed against
the sliding glass door while the sun held me flat
as my shadow evolved. Did you
cohabitate wisely? Once he shoved me into the bathtub.
There was an idol called Custom, this urged
certain truths onward. Unparticular and correct.

Come do it to me in person.

Idyll

A feather in a wire apparatus plus electronic exhaust
The rat and I in mutual cold

In which the sky proposes wisps of sky information
An old paralysis, you feel that?

These vast affairs with serious night
The old phases of love, someone sang of that

This casual involvement with the skin of profit
In a movement beyond art, come tell me that—

Of a lion's head and the beloved claw
Creation gathers my filth & your filth: we nod off in that corner

Down the hillside forms tumble
One passenger's common mistake, it was a curse

Out of the trash of the human poem
To think like that and with little acclaim

Into the gentle bobbing of thistle and candy
This could be a long tradition

Pleasurable scales of wheat lands & corn lands & edge
These former companions through the spider's web—

Lovely apple, cleo, phil
An intermittent childhood cannot tell us about clouds

Lovely apple, cleo, peach
And various tenting beauties of flowers

It was clearer how to mean to be alone
As convention inserts the presence of today

A few words, throw those down
In lush afternoon vocabulary, dreamy tender cover

They hunt us through the bitching forest
Today is nothing in the work of art

Spell

If the wizard loved you
he made you fat
he gave you
velvet and
possessions
Stupidly I supposed
he had written my life
as a periodic reality
a long yellow hurt
through the glade
A piece of angle iron
bent into plow
As dust and sun
blessing protests
then the fog—
hopeful, oblique
wary

Tho no one
believed in what
I was learning
a famous poet said
to her audience
there were gods
in Chicago
like a tone of voice
There weren't gods
or consensus
beyond the terrace
where we want

nothing to conceptualize
well. A carol in
the perfect wind
unfinished but alert—

The wizard added sweet time
Then he took it away

Through

Found the moment in a car,

next I lost it.

For the car is pierced by evil.

In a circle of patrons, on whom

might we inflict

such bright and minor status?

For reference, on May the 28th

some meteors came. Looking

is like hoarding

and thus hoarding. Try to move

beyond it, elongate the star sign

into a random object: crying baby.

Lord of the chest. And then

the salmon, agog.

Much insight is nonrecurring though

I would forage its source,

sever the crude future

of each weather. There is

a parallel shine

to one's conscience. It spins

its vinyl emotion

on some rooftop, like wind

the mixer. From the mud

comes the pattern. Moss,

struggle toward that yellow.

Where all one's fog lives

might be this softer institution,

a kind of people

and rawly uncreative, plus repetition:

I am attached to this bracelet.

I am attached to my carriage.

I am attached to such nectar.

The everyday guarantee

of certain visual diplomacy.

Put the cello on the spectrum,

put my essence. An ordinary moment,

no more gestures. Someone works

full-time in our error.

Other species. Or objects

worth discussing & above which

thorough cloudscapes hover.

I find myself outside their nuance,

leak away from all creeds.

What's wrong with right here?

Satisfaction is a plain destination.

As both woman & girl it nearly killed me.

The creeds claiming.

What's a manner

if not in theory. With a vine

across my back. Before light

could enter light turned

and denied us.

Get ahead of your pain

the ages counsel.

A fine pollen fell

through the world.

Make plenty of money.

Mansions

It's fall in the back of an Escalade
It was the middle of my thought
A beast expressed
A gallery opened
The whole ecclesiastical deal
Or little universals
But no synthesis

Smoothing pillar, silver clasp
And fillet—silver waves
The cherub in the golden courts
A child dragging a power cord
Original masses, one miniature dream
I have a love, I talk to them
Women digging with forks
Among the marriages
The not marriages
Now the jazz

Stay right with me—

Hearing those atoms
That muscle
And dirt
In the city
Of spirit

There's some natural education
In that sticker on the tree
In reality
What's back there?

Sirens, icons
Bacon, eggs

Not anything regular like a carrot
She peeled as she cried
From her broken face

Voice bright
After getting fucked
In a boring way

The full
Wet moon
An inch
Above me
And another inch
Of condos—

I drank a whole
I did a bunch

Viewed an ebill,
Dragged my foot:

The chronicle
Tells many lies
About change

Parable

One is flying,
walking, one is being wheeled.

One's sublet on this weedy earth,
one's improving cornucopia

or an apple bong
abetting one's conversion.

Whose name ended in gratitude
or confusion, which effects

led one to fiction, one
to works.

One is crying, one is
howling. One is burned

with the other. From the barrel
of our chair it was effort

then it was forgotten. It was like
a pearl of glue—one in one.

However one approached time
time was touchy.

There was weakness
shyness, wanting, dreams.

One's truth won't work in dreams, or in
real life it's confusing.

The most mythic duet
there is.

Who was least
no one wondered.

One is quieter
and never ceases to be.

This failure messes everyone
up. A whole revolution

arrived, did it happen
to this one born

regardless, who lived alone
—this one too—

or whose objects of survival
were one's cat, one's routines,

a dullsville book, some tea instead
of beer or vice versa.

It tore this one who heard.
It made this one a climate.

One was little, one older
one who got no older, one cried.

One becomes one but not others.
This failure happens again.

A whole revolution
tons of merit, of use to minors—

"how ill this describes
what it is like for us to alter"

One hinted at a rule
about the maimed

having thought
rather than hurt
one could make
one understand

A person sailing through the ether
an image pleading

Aging laptops beckoning
part to whole

Why one is reasonable
Why one unclear

Or there's some shitty pattern
in the pattern
discrediting one's party

As more powerful drugs ripped through
man's place in the world—

Could no longer hide
in that house of

No more cover
in the mental event

But the groin, the hair, the armpit: stack them together

Leave them
in the size of that—

One's face is heavy
One has no audience

Both feet were broken
it was birth

Then the choir

Earth

Nothing radical about that technology
Nobody touches this era

Could u find a home
Know my brother

Who has a mind too
Has a portion

Bucolic

It was a town and a factory
town they came from, it was earth
in a regular way no longer.
I moved Frances far from the river,
sure that the sentence
rots when no one is in it.
We go on talking, afloat
within the family substance.
No greater perfection, can you see
its basic, growing eye.
Descended on crystals.
Yard booming
new summer, I took away
the Vera irresolute at the edge.
Slid out of our past.
Ran the wrong summer,
began the idea on the side
of the water. It was the character
of apple, crab apple,
mulberry, horse.
The past a computer,
a wild computer. And two lights
from the porch meaning song
or direct quotes.
Disguised as a child
I address you.

Like this Carl who's rich
and the cousins then poor.
Other cousins are rich.
I am sure that voice is bad.
An uncle is dead,
a Louise. I can't really feel it,
the lantern under your shirt.
Another brother's cut off
but goes on living.
The bee on the grass
did a circular phrase.
There is that Viv.
Now she's ground yellow sticks.
That Stephanie, that Ruth.
Now there's a horizon
she's winging toward dead.

These circle me out—
the rich, the deformed.
Or without wanting to get into it
one got in. The middle
the platform, the lung.
Went into the orchard
alone I sat and thought
in the field, not mine
by the simple pronoun, not.
To remember our fight.
In the dark
there is no voice.
The simple answer is kindly.
Drank a coke
by the side of the town.

Plentitude matched only
by dreams and creatures
climbing that dream.
A daisy pattern,
at the end of belief.
Field directed after that
which has received it—
the cup of mint and
each branch.
Waved invitingly
over the pool.

Grace can't be read,
she's unavailable then.
The hoax inside the box.
All gold
in the yard.
Extending the river, table
of everyone sitting there,
all the plastic.
Then the quarrel rotted
on the table.
It wasn't charming
to cover the box with gardens.
Under windows and one
was named Chris.
Chris Chris.
How could I say it
in this age of improvement
that I decayed, that Carl?

From the frame Grace chooses
to speak: the church
had a face
it leaned out from.
The trees
went fine
in their light.
I never understood
the reason for my face.
The way it came up the road.
In the fields carry blight,
lime green of the water
and foam. Despite
our rugged name.
Or foam
of her lips. Face
in its church. He took
the machine. And she
the portrait. So far
no chemist could
locate them.

The Pencil

The teacher and the dune
Joined at the pencil

A crystal lattice in the darkened wood
Wild rhubarb jostling a lover's responsible letter

You had to be loose said the philosopher
From inside the cataract

Male secretaries devoted to their hand; the soul
Apologizing as it tags its sheep

That lavender heart
Buckled to an arm

Small tubes and barrels beget
Technical work and general writing and rare
Diamond loot, oh the queen despised it
For it had failed to sparkle

As shag upon cedar groves
Of Sweden, two rings on a desk
Lost in Budapest
Looking back on one's choices they form many rings

Many cloisters, a caption

The lining of the canon

Or a recluse walking through rain to god
Who is growing the business—

Its name, the biggest in the world
Coming through an unknown cursive
Long-legged and inappropriate, a tulip
Mist or waveform symbolizing agony and water

The leftist balladeering on the corner

Your arms scooping up the apex
To throw it down on paper

— The murderous history and wooziest image
A shipwreck! Plumbago
White buckets of latex —

A mean gang hunched
Beside the purple undertones of plants

Going

We were on
the Taconic Parkway

going south
through where Bard is

or not that far
not even

to Poughkeepsie
where Vassar is

not to where
it got wider

going through
the nettles

grasses and beech
the something

killing pine
for 45 minutes

then only 20 more
miles past

the cheap house
on pretty hills

blue mountains
beyond

the slicing road.
In Dutchess county

I considered my life.
Ownership

was impossible!
Enchantment

bent away
from the worm.

Law traveled
through gorges,

the ravines.
All wealth

disappeared
but into which

pocket? Two cabins
around a stump

trying for a
moral vocabulary.

An equivalent
of mind

emptied by apple
picking, plot.

It was good
in the dirt

though we didn't
judge

the dirt.
There was

a hawk
up there.

A woman
in a truck

just heroic.
There's some turtle

in the road. Birds
fat birds.

Years aloft
in the mirage.

A denser richer
inside or

a tangled
dark bush.

Froth, then pro
duction.

Downfall to own
and to not

said the traveler
from the edge

of the country.
Perfectly watchful,

a little bitchy.
His porch

where history dies
in a mouth

won't produce
a singing people.

One situation arrived.
An asbestos barn

arrived, tender
vehicle.

A black painted
awning, this injury

somehow related
to college.

Ability was bringing
these types

together and put
ting death

at the bottom.
Or walking through

one of those hanging
bead walls.

A million tattered
ripped chairs.

A sad face
and a smiley face.

Apprentices instructing
each other

in mimesis.
The visible being

one element
of its sentence,

nature planted
root vegetables

performed life
from memory.

Fed our molecules
to the vault

then history took
that mixture.

I wrote to you
from the common

crawling up
to an income.

You replied
that technique

contained
plenty, caught

the taxi
as it disappeared

from language.
And this collectible

spoon
from the former

democracies;
and that toddler

arranged fetchingly
around the drip

candles.
I'm really

brief
passing through.

Off by itself—
A drying rack.

A canoe no a kayak.
Jutting away toward

the house
in Dutchess county

I heard
your cough

from the outside
leaving

a task
unaccomplished.

Ode

Everything resounds in this wonderful trend
Every chemical substance upborne into my lungs
Each particular copy of war

Woke up dreaming of language, in texts
Of theory
Read a website

Do locomotive appeals in personal national crises
—These keys—
Explain me, individually

Does the unreadable symphony
Of the routine

I run my hand along its thigh

I go adroit within its canopy
Trying to find my Grecian state
My love of perfected repose
In the bodega's debris

Sleep, to the stars, rocks, mountains, and jobs
To the student interpreter of rare, extravagant shit
To the episode, the tripod, the priest—

This one's a bold stroke in blunt language
This doodle, an old reformer

This perfectly nat-u-ral text
I am sending
Bout this ivy
Hogging brick

And of its concealment
I'll paraphrase:

I like to walk in the sun
He hacked

I like to pass
The clothes drop dumpster

I like to kneel
Before the waterfall

Virtue Theory

"A moral philosophy should be inhabited"
        —Iris Murdoch

Thirty four years + almost one month
                minus pen with working pen
I cook myself lots of dinners.
        scratches on my knee from raspberry picking today

        out with my brother
                at the bookstore and he asked me up
        to see his place twice.

In a year he'll hardly talk to me.   is he able, terrible, did
proportions   produce the pain.
                        or it's one complicated phrase
        extending from multiple mistakes.

Drinking too much by the baby
loving the balcony and city   its appropriate quartet, joy
        and friendship   orgasms, cash.
            grabbing stuff in honor of the past

            hoping it will all flash recognizably again—it's a
    problem

            for every art coming from outside   and
        inside too, I guess nobody wants
        what they can't hear.   a specific tortured look

in one video, noise from the frame.   how about Willa Cather
writing about wolves,
        inner static or—a real suspicion
            re the whole idea.

not even a rhythm
or too much rhythm it doesn't go around
the neighbors.   a trope I saw that was
a landscape   t-shirt   blanket   printed w/boobs
8 cats 12 babies.   an organizing
system

in the meaning of tones, half-tones,   neighbors fighting
then laughing   or crying is laughing.

"since labour though useful, is itself a punishment"
(St. Augustine)

a triple longing, remoteness   but w a grown-up feeling
of endurance and practice. blueish smoke without intention.
the sound of them
having sex while I have none.

wake up thinking   what a thought of finance, what a
        moody morning being the right age.

            was alive   going up the stairs
for a little exercise   moving my spine.
        wasn't as excited as I should have been
                about the book inside the book. felt as though
                        living was dying, one story died,
reappeared as an email.   two portraits
        in this space—a lighter—keys. dead phone, dead light,
        redolent swains.

"I had but one sister
And I have been her dead"
(The Milk White Doe)

horse threw him   the son cut off her head

               they were sung
          who loved a ballad
                              but too well

Eildon tree beside the cell tower
                at the junction of whatever
                and the beautiful.
        junction of potato, cow.   anthem
her brother   made in the year
made wrong from him.

coming down the road.
        one death by horse—universal.
                        an outside force/circumstance
        then the rule   a kind of pattern
        no gold inside.   true lovers. wrapped
as a swain.
for we'll never etc.

                    "She went to the garden
                        To pull the leaf aff the tree" (Mary
                    Hamilton)

"He turned his face   unto the wall"
        Barbara Allen's cruelty

                        printed in his face

was ten miles from town without any money
      meaning   hell was observable:
           description / gesture
           events, object language,
     to discard my metalanguage @ moments /
bring it to bareness   flowers   thorns
      growing out of graves   children dead men lovers
      basic shit   at the gate.

the world is thick but uncertain. one spear
        traveled as   a weapon   a dick   "it is all
                very real, medieval, and pioneer." (Gertrude
                Stein)

        who could find arcadia, speak—
                        a private impossibility   youth
                my eggs skin cells contributing to dust
        the New American anything.

everyone crawls away   from the voice. in this
        a species of modernist thought, belief.
        here's a complication   the perceived world can't fill
me in on,   can't put it in
        poem-wise, that sense of intimacy and death.
        politesse—

        weeping in a room with some tea and a candle
              it wasn't supposed to be this way,
        turn out this way, maybe it was.
              —intermittently tuned—

        hiding in a rural place—and then
        being born—

"New emotions: humility: impersonal joy: literary despair"
(Virginia Woolf)

reading Woolf's diary   rooting for her,
hoping for a new   fantasia

I came earnestly before a hut.
washed up. there would be the possibility
to be as a cheetah or leopard
      an apple, the game
      give me residence plz I'm silently
      a little worse than I appear.

inventing a language or being in bed.
in the environment of time
a human wish   a handicap.

the meeting in which
he did a number   she replied
there were plants, a particular smell   like incense
it was incense and heat unnecessarily.
it was a wild one, the spring   the fall.

sentences that wouldn't write themselves.
as a memory of humiliation   tickles, descends.
carry it off   was one instruction.
bury it, bone it, bring it along.

Bright!   bright and cold   calamitous.

blurry as,

and younger   more insignificant,
a joke.

really work each instant   it's coming through
into the frame   or lying now
        on one's back with a whimper
                he will never know you
                        the caretaker said in a mourning way.

anyone's breakfast table   on a given morning. anyone's
        student describing in depth
                their visual imagination.
        to understand oneself
                sentiment's already gone before—there's
                genres there—

do you know
        where you are when you write a thing?
        in the middle of the parterre.

through the walls my neighbors talk
      I am always trying to get a poem from this
they give out tones   laughter   sex.
      a door opens etc.
      feels both behind   curiously inside me
         as though I was my room   their place

this bug.   what's true
          his body would decay
the muscles   his foot   not my foot.

we were painting in my kitchen
and she would say no more
about the house of siblings.   but in what fashion
        by which mechanism
                holding together many factual questions

of public life   or being together
        was the first of these his voice
                very excited then a quick stutter   he's hiding
for a sec   then he's proud.

        I live another life in my brother's voice.
                when he wrote me he was dying did
I understand.   what's the same
                                as what—a defect,

some limit   the materials   all one has.
        they stopped the line   have the memory
                maybe keep this cable.

muffled

    drilling

       dragging
          overhead, renovating
on a Friday afternoon.   looked hard at him

    my neighbor
       on whom I'd based many lines.

what's the mood?

    intermittent grandeur
summer autumn   and eternal schemes.

> "he had no housen there,
> ne anie covent nie" (Thomas Chatterton)

I had a sense that all the seed caps hanging on the porch even as a
child arranged our family via troubled economies, displays.
when I moved back here my brother went—it wasn't my fault
but I was reading that schizophrenia might liberate us from
capitalism. it was noble to read the long

chapters. because delusion itself is a hole filled with

language, somehow I arrived a little less to myself, less and less,
stepping into the pages without mind. his talking crawled through
its struggle uglier and hurt inching toward. had an angry voice that
stopped the extent within me, around me, ordered him one night
on a corner through my

phone. no basis was demonstrated not the conspiracy of

dates and where the letter had been stamped. not gender, the
religion of family, where I would die lying as the one born who
wrote a book, he said, a singular someone more true, more ill,
disabled in the reign of technology, my

government. on the corner, around.

maybe it's the millennials   compassionate
       and identical, moving
              there is no argument
                   regarding May.

      been reading
            this was supposed to last
                for eternity.

all theories of life   now breached   whereas
     we.   come from nowhere.
        it's a commune.

just back from dance   —peculiar to come out
        of noise not knowing how
                to get the brain straight.
just back from dance

                        where we lay on the floor
        let yourself sink
                as the one woman entered   I had zero
ideas   coming from the overlapping
        surfaces—horrible to be up there,
                part of it all   only   and zilch.
imagine the music's coming on   it's "Brew Fest"
        someone's scratching

                it's coming from that clump of trees,
a busy   irresponsible afternoon.   could you tear
the socket between us   reinstall
        lie back   let my joints open.

        walked quietly it was 6:30-7:15.
        I think it's a very thin atmosphere,
                the freedom of art
                not fragile but thin.
                there's enough of us
                by the dump.

suppose as I've said
        it's an attempt
                at the thinness of experience no
I mean occurrence, poem
        vacations where one travels
                via service

to an attitude.   how thin states predominate—pale, in
        decay of the robust
        historical imagination
            where I'm composing every song
of praise and blame   to a heavy French bass.

        such was the narrator who missed the point
          of narrative,   thereby increasing our
respect for the poet.   bribery was my figure.

        hides, skins, and wool.

the conversation in which he came at her
from beyond the barrier
      low sounds of theory,   friend in the wall.

        take on the experience of space—mood
atmosphere   you'll soon find the world
     a series of closed, self-enclosing chambers.

      printed material
of a strong young woman   on her knees
    in the granary, arms raised   in rhetoric, parsons
approach.

      an original poet
        printed off in duplex,
           small formal soul.
  do you believe in the natural environment also?

      lazy cycle, wear it down.
      disappear
          into a little skit
called human artifice.

    action in our common life,
      action in bed. that's fine.

lead us to the 28th century
      where space has mastered time
            which is never "lived"
but entered   army-style.

     being like himself but also   so unlike himself.
repealing this fascination   a funny voice spoke through
me
       literally funny + obscene.

                someone affected an accent we were discussing
therapeutical methods. she went
to the shamanism class   I met my conveyer there
                at the blushing edge.
                        a cabin   with a blanket
                                       over the windows
pure possibility.
                        into the pastures
at dusk   climbing up
                one of the old horses

                                with a sense of vastness, yearning
for all times   in all times—

                I was unlocatable there.
        that felt good.

                and to speak of certain
cousins who were dirty   from work   didn't wear shoes
        country stories   games   routines

                                in which play was
        possible   didn't interrupt work
                but existed alongside it.

actually
        various, surprising

communal   permeable   full
of animals   wandering

      strangers arriving in cars

looking for someone
   then stay for a spell   taking over
someone's hand, playing a round, heading out.

supercontingent.
a shaggy personable aspect.
spoiled myths.

'd like to tinker with matter
        this poem'll do.

                        would like to live
out there   all alone   to water
        make good

                grow a thing
                        not a child
                        not corn.

bc categories are broad,
    banal and one languishes
        in the colossus because
        the split level determines
    a particular practice   I am guided

    by some iota of history
it's not art / or very typical.   it's typical to try.
    walk out into the precise names
    of fertilizer
        lye on the field.

last night in this hotel.
        but the air is cool it's night.   haven't
responded   where it all happened
    and then I learned.   there were words,
        he was gone

   .

        then the hard tile
            put my bed upon. all sorrow
through him.   not mine   but all
    but the world
        won't bow
        to my brother good night.

say I'm a little more liquid   on the day John Ashbery
          dies. a hummingbird
                          sips from the whatnot
fluted   next to my ear.
              you need 500–1000 dollars
                          to fix all kinds of lack.

saw Hazel in a dream walking up the gravel
    a little dog with her.
        it was hot, she carried a hanky.
wearing her same old   sleeveless button-up.
        moving slow but steady on.

      watched her from the old porch, idly
        and before the dream.

      like art.

reading spatial theory   in the sublet w beer.
          grey couch and bar
              I broke observations on,
                drying shit on the car outside.
          would never write   how he sat
                could scarcely look
flinched his wide thumb   thick brows.
          it was on his face I thought.
                his rage   in all respects
              all wrong for them,
          won't work for them.
throbbing need that doesn't know itself
          can't name itself.
                in his odd body, stuck face.

the wind comes up your coat, the streets are too long, the
distribution's unfair, people freeze, don't take their meds, drop out
of high school, talk through their nose.
                                                    it's in yr
mind in the middle, being trapped, they kill Black people here, it's
always school. you come across hunters, birds shit on the cars,
I'm embarrassed a lot, feel compelled to

respond. the lake's stupid, the Art Institute's expensive, there are
no mountains, beyond boring, the families come from farms, it's all
I can remember now. what can you

remember about it. once it was marsh.

tried to get on my mitten   glove combination.
          pushed my thumb through.
                    enjoyed the bad pop music
                              changed radio channel 4-7 times,
drove around.   combed hair with hand, waited,
          scraped gunk   from mouth corner, moved my toes,
noticed new hairstyle on stylist   she gave a fake
smile.   played with ring.
          cold hand under sweater
                    on warm shoulder, tilted head back,
shifted weight   let a tear fall   beamed outward
          abashedly looked to the ground.
          placed hands in air.
          dried toothbrush.
          flapped hand in the sink   to spread water

                    around also chemicals.
                    bent an elbow   curled
          hand at wrist under my chin, reclined.
          held beer in left hand then right index finger around neck,
put hand at back of neck to feel.   extracted

          card from wallet slid across counter.
          pointed at dog in a sweater
          in a dream said
                    that's not a human child.

rotated feet poorly in boots,   "squared" shoulders.
          curved fingers around opposing textures.
                    pushed thumb down   to erase attention.
lifting chin   through recent changes.
          curved more fingers   drawing one down
                    through boredom. took chemical into hand
delightedly.   opening hand around mouth
          spreading concentration.
                    isosceles triangling
with one hand   chewing nail   wondering.
          rubbing the week.
                    caring for time.   curling fingers.
arching fingers   upon hurting products.
          reading "words are difficult to put into words."

at this point he'd stopped texting, had never answered, was he
working or freaking out.
      at times the soulhead is hollow, flat, demeaned. what was
      he doing now,
           pursuing the clock
               sitting with a machine.
    "Our stings are our destiny" (Iris Murdoch)

      I'm devoted to you,
           these energies,
what comes through   the inner
inside song   celestial.

      I'm devoted to you.

"I bought a ballad of one who was singing it in the street, because I thought it was written on me." (William Cowper)

blizzard in which the city reorganizes

belonging.   reading Cowper

    fail at suicide. are you

    in the red parka with fur trim

      or the grey?

        how can argument   go on

when everyone's so crazy sad?   what are the day's

    developments, who put another woman

      on a bus in their poem.

"A vein of self-loathing and abhorrence ran through all his insanity" (Robert Southey)

first light he saw   in days

    striping the memorial gardens.

so clear expression   made you nervous.

    but look   at reality. how do we

    want to live.

ruffled tops   of window drapes.
        he pushed the world   thus n away.
                could there be a way to inhabit
a moral philosophy w out being annoying about it?

                so it showed,   you knew it,
                        but expected little
        were richly rewarded.   doing away

                with the parts that are most I am
        in the library   under ruffled windows
                maybe it's a high old tone

                        after all.   virtue theory.

—as though action passed   through us
          wind or light,
          energy,
     maybe just money,
                    went on while we stood
     a cracked sidewalk   next to some park,
          mom dragging her kid by the arm.
these were the sights   underneath flowed
     truth beyond syntax. it was no image
                    had no president   spun our brains.
the exciting early days   of blogs—

     proud striving toward the puppeteer.
 casually sorting   one's predicaments.
     words like bodies, or cells,

shadow tension   directing the keystrokes.
                    no topic
               but happiness of animation here.
          humanities   and solitudes.
leathery leaves, undersides red
          overside green   red at the edge.
                    potted and pots   placed in chips,
          a sunken bed of chips.
                    before the leaves   a finger
dark crimson,   alive and ignored.
               prob 5-7 feet of them.

'd like to finish this book
       these specific years.
           that slow gel
             it ate of we   and deserved it.
someone typed   at someone else.
        —doing menial labor among the screens.

       he cruises up   in his Accord

but the world's dead this day I eat a scone,

       there's ten computers,   guy

          on a break.

"the transformation of a maiden
　　　into a bird
　　　　　by some jealous person."
　　　mom singing Polly Vaughn
　　　　　could I love her, The Fowler

on the Shooting of his Dear.
　　　"paltry stuff," "a silly ditty."

　　　　　Laurel Brooks née Speer sang
in a VW camper bus　　　　　a Ford Explorer
　　　in the late 1980s　　　　　c. early and mid 90s.
　　　　　this was at night
to keep herself awake on cross country drives
　　　sometimes made in anger or distress.

　　　　　her singing bothered her son
which was　　　　　or should have been
　　　a sign of what

　　　　　　　　　to whom.
　　　"one of the very lowest descriptions of vulgar modern
English ballads."　　　　　hated, envied,
　　　　　killed with a magic gun.
　　　turning from nothing to something.
young in the rain.
　　　　　"shallow and silence."
　　　our names meant drunk and barren.　　　　　whose
children inherit the earth.

Poetry

Come out of your program, we're all poolside
Amongst the nature imagery

Come honor the particularized salon, its endurance
Of the jailor. The judge
And the amputee

For this utopian gesture, for this vanity publisher—

A man stood next to his heart
His exclamation point, his kisses and hugs
Produced as an autumn day
Entering the world

The mirror is majestic and raw and just
Like biology

Like one of those long country roads
With a party at the end
A person in casual shoes

Walking to their local meaning

A broken orange
Settled on the mud

In my pragmatism we were covered up with
And I was never—

In the future I'll
In the future I'll populate
And be inexpert

On fringes
Full of asymptotes
And glamorous phrasing, and inclusive
Of singular emotions
In constant aesthetics
Where I'm watching the sources
Of funding

The empty plastic waters
Car horn, sparrows, and Cointreau
One squirrel in the past's penetrating magic

What is the true relation between numbers
And tears? A birch in a pot before a TV

Apocryphally, the woman
Called it off we think with her sadness

I have loitered
That old maneuver

And into which typographical struggle
From which recurrent psychosis did I go on
Turning, this irresponsible shuffle

This hoo-hoo-hoo
Of my various triumphs,

Capitol

Magic circle of horses   + magic funicular.
      heaps of stuff being sold.

      freedom   to trace this petty action.
where do we   go now?

floated up there along you   abandoning you
who was able
      for better floating, our living

      + one mother's voice,   magic little river.
      heaps of stuff being sold.

       the ones who seemed like dicks like Michelangelo
or just "consummate artists"—
vegetables   out
on the ground.

dogs chilling in their roundabouts.

      so it was coming   from the corn
         the sun prairies   to the maze / to the faces
without haloes   .

the wing yellow into white   + yellow mint.
motif of garden or pocket

while the fog rolls in no
magic from the bunker

         or what's coming but magic

                    said she
                    to be alive
at all. the earth

plunged in
        into rooms.

while they worked in shops,
            made something we would call clog or carved
messages to outer space

                    upon boxes of varying dimensions.
                    involved their bodies and bodies
of children   in apparatuses

for days or weeks or years.
+ from obscure movements   sent out trinkets,

            clothing, God.
            when he died everyone paused
            to take a little stock,
                    his brief remarks were read aloud.

        energetically the dark converses

like magic the
casino.   carousel + empty
pyramid.

            metal barricades, old country baroque
            music + lithium.
            long walk for food.

"the future is hidden." (Kropotkin)
as one retires to her quarters
the narrative gathers power   + people remain.
          meander
through blood.   deciding between

the social goods. "meaning and confusion
are both beautiful." (Goodman)

          + late at night or the mean cashier
old markets   where a general idea of many
          became sick
                    unto the reality of one.
                    the turquoise tarp

housing some pigeons.

          that property   of the baron's,
                    still there on the moon.

Acknowledgments

Thank you to Ingrid Becker, Dan Bevacqua, Peter Gizzi, Emily Hunt, Mark Leidner, Gwen Muren, and Sara Nicholson for comments and guidance. Thanks to Wong May for her words and poems. Thank you to my Location workshop students at the University of Chicago, winter 2018. Ben Estes and Alan Felsenthal, my especial thanks to you.

Unattributed quoted language in "Parable" and "Virtue Theory" is from Iris Murdoch.

Versions of some of these poems first appeared in *Banango Street, Dreginald, Fence, Heir Apparent, The Journal Petra, jubilat, Pinwheel, Poetry Now, Tupelo Quarterly,* and *West Branch.* Sincere thanks to the editors of these journals.

OTHER TITLES FROM THE SONG CAVE:

1. *A Dark Dreambox of Another Kind* by **Alfred Starr Hamilton**

2. *My Enemies* by **Jane Gregory**

3. *Rude Woods* by **Nate Klug**

4. *Georges Braque and Others* by **Trevor Winkfield**

5. *The Living Method* by **Sara Nicholson**

6. *Splash State* by **Todd Colby**

7. *Essay Stanzas* by **Thomas Meyer**

8. *Illustrated Games of Patience* by **Ben Estes**

9. *Dark Green* by **Emily Hunt**

10. *Honest James* by **Christian Schlegel**

11. *M* by **Hannah Brooks-Motl**

12. *What the Lyric Is* by **Sara Nicholson**

13. *The Hermit* by **Lucy Ives**

14. *The Orchid Stories* by **Kenward Elmslie**

15. *Do Not Be a Gentleman When You Say Goodnight* by **Mitch Sisskind**

16. *HAIRDO* by **Rachel B. Glaser**

17. *Motor Maids across the Continent* by **Ron Padgett**

18. *Songs for Schizoid Siblings* by **Lionel Ziprin**

19. *Professionals of Hope*, The Selected Writings of **Subcomandante Marcos**

20. *Fort Not* by **Emily Skillings**

21. *Riddles, Etc.* by **Geoffrey Hilsabeck**

22. *CHARAS: The Improbable Dome Builders*, by **Syeus Mottel**
    (Co-published with Pioneer Works)

23. *YEAH NO* by **Jane Gregory**

24. *Nioque of the Early-Spring* by **Francis Ponge**

25. *Smudgy and Lossy* by **John Myers**

26. *The Desert* by **Brandon Shimoda**

27. *Scardanelli* by **Friederike Mayröcker**

28. *The Alley of Fireflies and other stories* by **Raymond Roussel**

29. *CHANGES: Notes on Choreography* by **Merce Cunningham**
    (Co-published with the Merce Cunningham Trust)

30. *My Mother Laughs* by **Chantal Akerman**